Catch And Release

text and illustrations
by sarah van arsdale

Finishing Line Press
Georgetown, Kentucky

Copyright © 2024 by Sarah Van Arsdale
ISBN 979-8-88838-670-5   First Edition
All rights reserved under International and Pan-American Copyright Conventions. No part of this book may be reproduced in any manner whatsoever without written permission from the publisher, except in the case of brief quotations embodied in critical articles and reviews.

Publisher: Leah Huete de Maines
Editor: Christen Kincaid
Artwork: Sarah Van Arsdale
Author Photo: Peter Bricklebank

Order online: www.finishinglinepress.com
also available on amazon.com

Author inquiries and mail orders:
Finishing Line Press
PO Box 1626
Georgetown, Kentucky 40324
USA

For my brother, Peter Van Arsdale,
who first introduced me to the study
of natural history

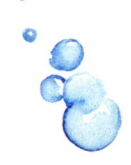

Long ago, I heard that nurse sharks swim
far below the surface of the sea,
sedentary, slow,
by day clustering in a waltzy, sleepy thrum,
resting in the ledges of the undertide.

    At night they suckle through the shallow seabed flats
                                          for their living prey.

Could this be true—

that sunk
beneath the gull-flocked sky
the white caps' fall and rise
below the surface-feeding fish
the strands of spinning seaweed,

submerged beneath the undertow
down where the coral reef
regenerates and breathes,

this secret creature lives
square-jawed, pickle-brown, slippery—
not meant for you or me,
at twilight rousing, a rush of seafloor sand
rising in a sudden spray?

Even though we'd always said
Cancun was a place we'd never go
—*too touristy,
not the real Mexico*—
the flight there was direct, and, for us,
relatively cheap.

At the carousel we got our bags,
immediately swarmed by guys
in tidy polo shirts and shorts
calling out, in English, tours by boat or car,
to see the ruins of the Mayan empire,
Chichen Itza or Tulum
or to swim with sharks,
close to the hotels.

On the ferry deck, above the water's churn and thud,
a man played bamboo pipes for tips—
the tired tune I think of as a Paul Simon hit,
though I know that it's Peruvian.

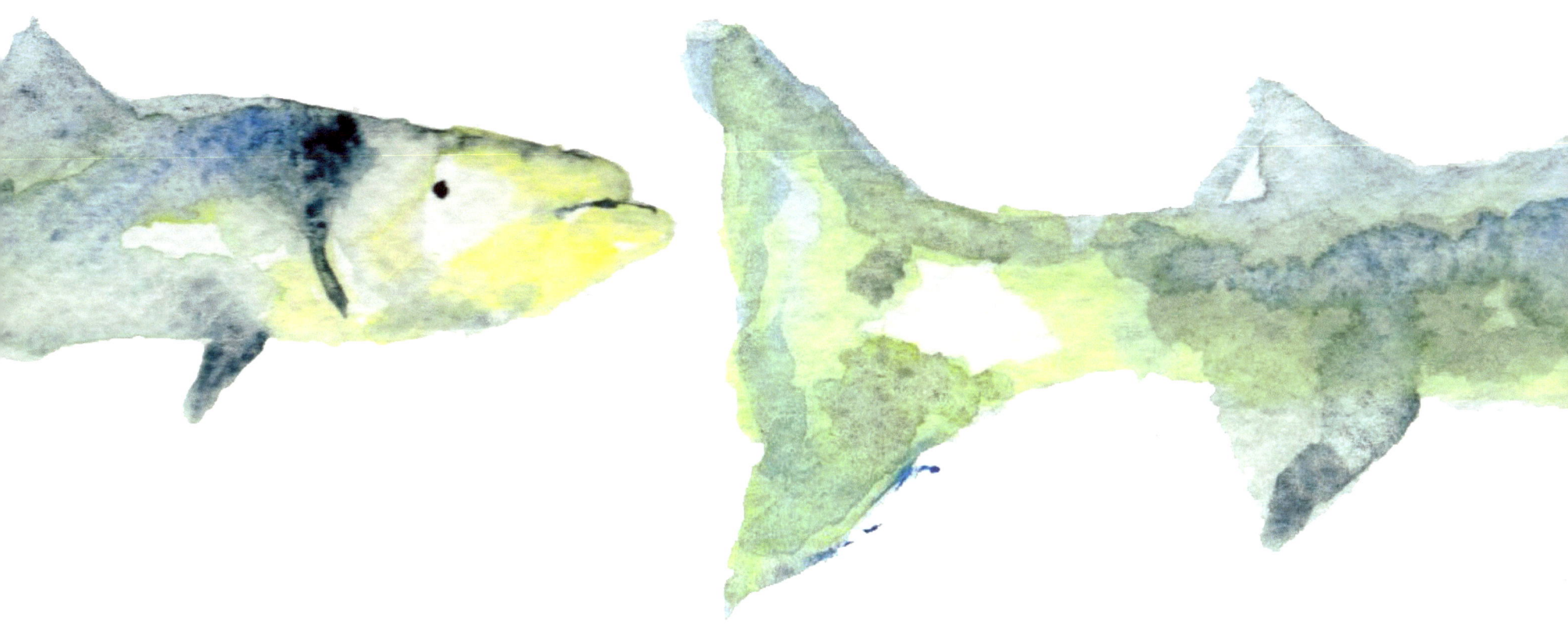

The notes lifted into the salty spray,
almost sailing my heart too
all the way to the island, a smudged
horizon line
of crystal peacock green.

We released our soiled paper masks
to the wind and gulls,
laughing because we'd gotten out,
and the island waited with its promise of a different world,
if only for five days.

There would be few tourists,
and parti-colored fish to see,
offering us some relief.

The world as it had been, before all this.

We'd been told the island was an oasis
from the herd of tourists
marching up the world's palisades and shores,
trudging through the ruins of an older, also
ruined world.

(There are so many climbers on Everest,
we'd read,
they have to form a line of hundreds
on the ridge,
scrambling in the icy snow,
with their dome tents, altimeters,
harnesses and ropes.
Oxygen intake low, temperatures of 2 below.
Some die that way, stumbling in the crowd
or pushed off to the side.)

On this island
we'd be free of the crush of our own kind.
There were hardly any cars allowed,
just bikes, and golf-carts
repurposed for the sandy roads.

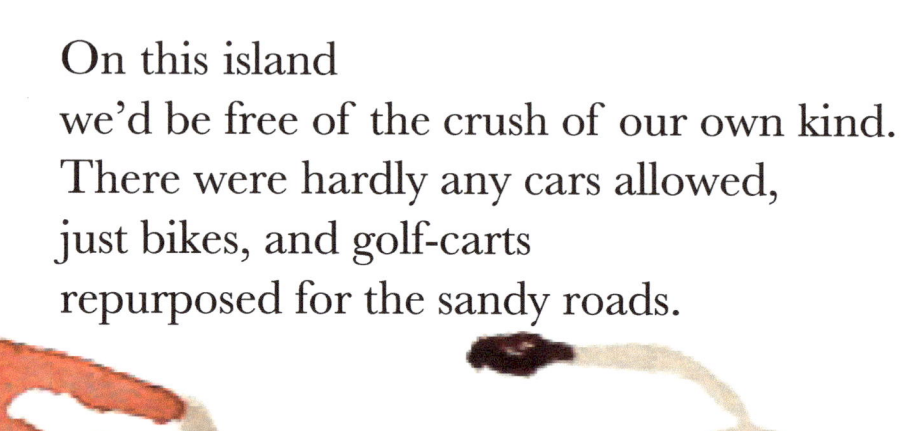

And in the sea, our hearts would lift to see fish silvering along the coral reefs: *great fish*, we were told.

Before we came, back at dismal home,
when my nightmares abated and I simply dreamed,
I dreamed of them, the colors surging
from the coral reef, like I'd seen years ago
when I was young,
along a different coast of Mexico.

The first day, I strapped my flippers on
and grasped the plastic tube between my lips.
Flippered, masked, I dove into the turquoise sea,
hovered over stoplight parrotfish,
a flock of palm-sized sergeant majors
schooling me.
Weightless, no longer bound
by gravity or guilt or grief.

Alone, just me, my respiration
and my heartbeat. The catch of my breath,
and its release.
Systole, diastole.

And yet.
My heart didn't rise and spill
the way it used to do.

The reef seemed dulled to the sepia
of old photographs,
(my grandmother holding down her hat
in the winds of Guatemala or Belize).
I was sure the colors
had been brighter blues and greens,
fluorescent cobalt and staghorn coral washed
with other-worldly, unnamed hues.

Was it the world, or was it me?
The world made not fresh, but new
by all our exploration,
our yearning to see the snowy view from Everest
or to watch porpoises
leaping through the inky blue.
Now so far removed from our own natural, dying habitat
we enter the forests and the seas
to press our ears against pulse of earth
but still get home in time for drinks.

                                                Me, too.

I dove into the waters in my human body,
with my plastic flippers and my mask,
wrecking as I did
the very things I want to see survive.

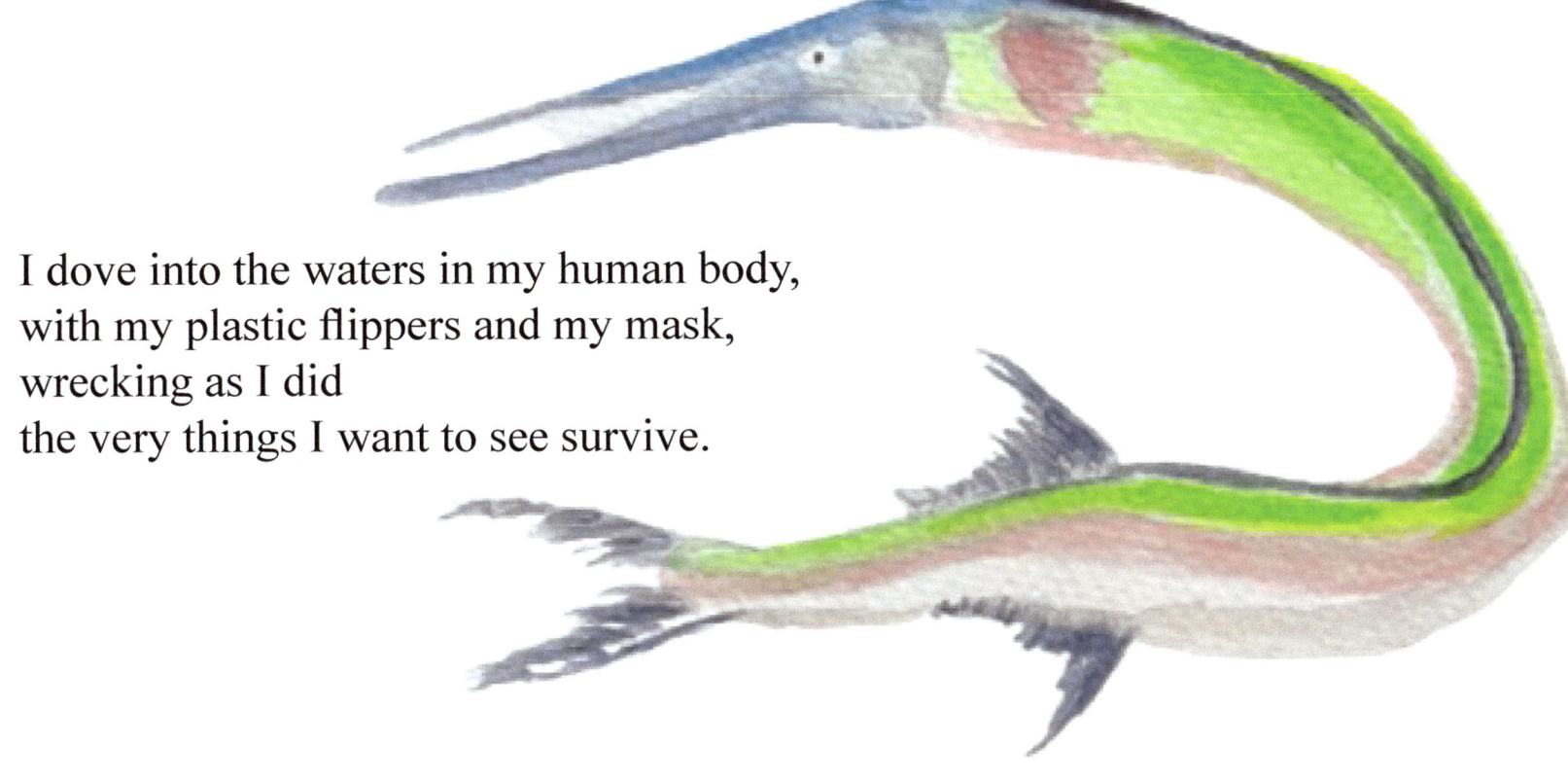

On the island's busy northern tip,
one afternoon
I argued with the man
—stocky, with terracotta skin—
who rented us a golf cart
that broke down in the rain,
stranding us at the southern beach.
I saw myself as if from up above:
a white woman,
embittered, fortunate,
fed up, near tears.

Near tears, that's how I've felt
these last three years, watching the world
plummet toward a place
I never thought I'd see.
The plague's still here,
the refugees in weakened boats.
Do I need say any more?
The fires on the California coast. The drought at home.
The panic tapping on the windows
as I draw the curtains closed.

What I am isn't what I thought I'd be.

The nurse shark is known for what's called
"site fidelity," meaning it likes to call a certain place
in the seagrass flats or mangroves home,
returning to that undersea ridge that's known.

Its docile lumbering makes it vulnerable
to spears thrown from motorboats
or to the churning blades of cruises
with their guides and open bars.
The gillnets and the longlines, the poisonous parabens
in our sunscreen and the water
ever warmer every year.

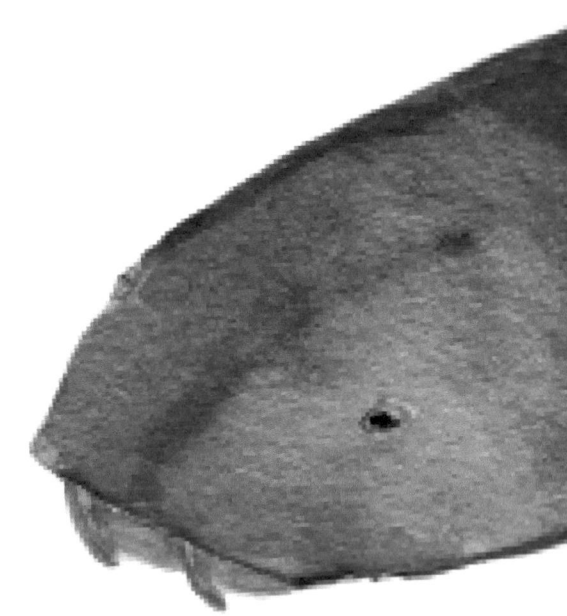

Our third day on the island,
we learned the protected reef far off the coast
was closed.
I wasn't sure I understood,
my Spanish being faulty, full of holes.
No, the man said, *it's really closed.*
El arrecife está ciertamente cerrado.

No tours, no boats, due to a bacteria
the scientists still don't understand
and the change in climate,
and the tourists, with our flippers
and our parabens,
our need to swim too close.

Is it forgivable that I want
to gasp in awe at everything,
to try and catch a glimpse
of a Cassin's finch or pillar coral
or a shark, before they disappear?
Or, before I die?
To lay my palm against
the flank of something wild,
wild as I wish I were?

The day before we left, I took a tour boat
to a smaller reef, closer in,
and swam among the swarming fish.
If I wanted, I could fit one in
my palm.
I was lost in them,
like being lost in love-making
when I was young and anything seemed possible,
my breath loud and regular
as if I'd swallowed down the rhythm of the sea.

Back on board, we were ferried to the shore,
passing swaths of sea grape and oleander,
the wild blooming naupaka trees
that drop their fruit into the sea.

Half-buried in the sand, an abandoned kayak,
the fibers of its frame
weakened by the years of salt and sea.
The tour ended at a dock,
bordered with palms and devil's ivy.

When we disembarked I saw a crowd,
hunched by the rail
as if at a crime scene
or an accident.

I looked too.

In the water, beside the dock,
a dark-skinned man—likely Mayan, but he could have been
from anywhere in Mexico—
held an enormous, passive creature in his arms.
Had it been wounded?
Was he keeping it from harm?

                              Then I saw the tourists, one by one,
                              ladder from the dock into the water of the pen,
                              to have their picture snapped,
                              as if by the side of a celebrity.

Click, click, click.
The cameras on the cell phones whirred and ticked
and the shark accepted it,
resigned, beyond despair.

I didn't stay for lunch.

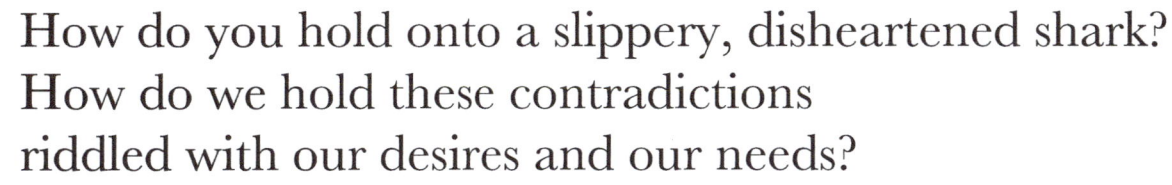

How do you hold onto a slippery, disheartened shark?
How do we hold these contradictions
riddled with our desires and our needs?

That night, I couldn't sleep, the sea so close
in its churn and thud.
The island's northern end
weighted with those big hotels,
all the paving and the golf-carts,
the restaurants and bars
sinking in the pink-white sand.

And the nurse shark, lying in the murky water
of her pen, dreaming of her seagrass flats,
the ridgeline of her coral reef,
knowing the next day will bring
another line of humans
to have their way with her.

As the moon rose and night descended to the sea
was she bewildered by her throttled need to swim and feed
through salt-starred water,
to fly over a riot of orange and seal-coat blue,
swimming elegantly underneath the waves
through clouds of fish and waving weeds,
hearing, as I was in our rented bed,
the sea tides' roll and thrum,
and longing to escape?

Sleepless, too, I rise and slip
from bed, find the pliers and the saw
I bought that day in town.
Herramientas, I'd learned to say.
I pull on my sweatshirt
And close the door.

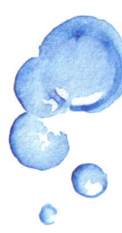

The night is battened down
by cloud and fog.
Flashlight in one hand,
I follow my private circle of light
until the skies clear
and I can see the fronds of palms
etched, stuttering against the clearing sky.

Dogs bark, far off, as I approach
the restaurant, now shuttered, dark.
I don't bother with the metal gate,
but shoulder in, between the fencing
and the seagrape, and soon I'm on the beach,
at the old kayak I saw that afternoon.
Beneath the weary hull, a single paddle
as if it had been left there just for me.

In the boat, I near the dock
thinking of the guard, a trigger-happy kid
hired to protect the prisoner.
But there's just the waves against the hull.
The dock takes shape in the dark,
the ribs of the pen rising from the water
a palisade of misery.
I paddle hard against the tide, and crouching low
I disembark.

In the murky water, I can see
her mysterious, thick shape
silvered by the moon,
nocturnal beast forced to still herself
while the night sea rolls and roils
out there beyond her cage.

I slip down the steps; the water's colder
than it was by day, and there's a film of slime;
it's hard to keep my grip.
The shark stays away; she wants nothing
to do with the likes of me.
I find a spot where I can stand and prise
my pliers in between
the wooden slats. There isn't any give at first,
and then one pulls free so suddenly
I fall back, go under with a salty slap,
then rise back up, baptized in turbid sea.

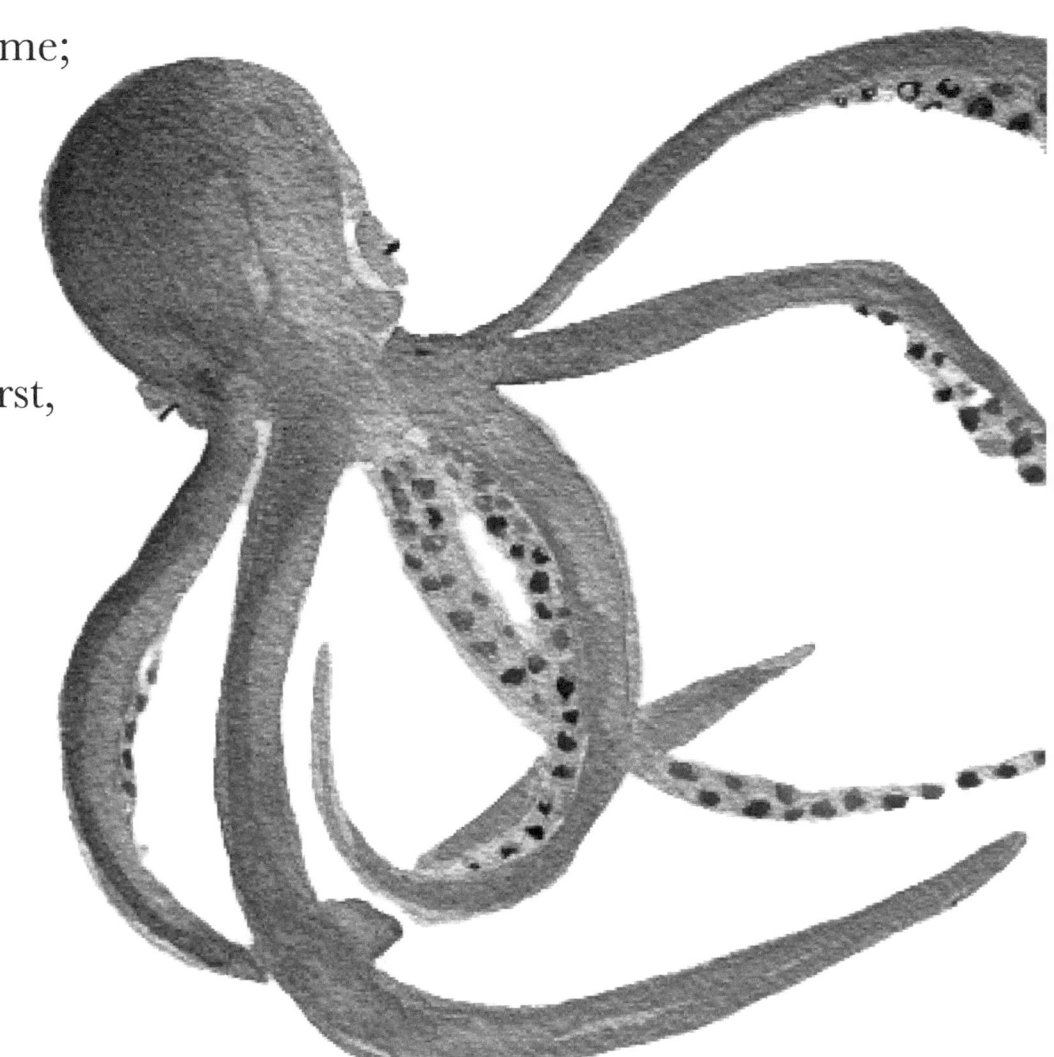

I can see so little here: just the curving fin,
the animal bewildering, leaning close
against her side of the pen.
I find the wire fencing and I cut. And prise again.
The sky is will soon be lightening the sea's dark shoulder

—and my heart, my heart, alive—

Suddenly, it's done. The wood must be weak
from years of soaking in the brine.

She doesn't look at me.
Initially, she's hesitant,
then rises from the shallow sandy floor,
swims through the gate I've made.

Her slipstream ribbons out into the sea.

Acknowledgments

Thanks, everybody, for whatever you're doing to encourage art and writing, and for your efforts to protect the vulnerable. Thanks, as ever, to my community of writers and artists for the abiding encouragement, the arduous mountain hikes, and the deep dives.

For this book, I'm especially indebted to Ilyas Iliya for his design ideas, Rachel Morton for insisting on redemption, Dorothea Osborn for expanding my understanding of watercolor, and Peter Bricklebank for telling me to make this story a poem—and for always helping me keep my head above water.

And an ocean of thanks to everyone at Finishing Line Press.

Resources

Reef Renewal International
https://www.reefrenewal.org
A global network of coral restoration programs.

Daughters of the Deep
https://daughtersofthedeep.org
An international organization seeking equal opportunities for women in marine science.

Centro Mexicano de la Tortuga
https://www.gob.mx/conanp/acciones-y-programas/centro-mexicano-de-la-tortuga
Based in Oaxaca, Mexico, an organization protecting sea turtles.

Sarah Van Arsdale is a writer and illustrator. Her sixth book, *Taken*, a poetry collection, was published in 2021 by Finishing Line Press. She is the author of four books of fiction: *Toward Amnesia* (Riverhead, 1996), *Blue* (winner of the Peter Taylor Prize for the Novel, University of Tennessee Press, 2003), *Grand Isle* (SUNY Press, 2012), and *In Case of Emergency, Break Glass* (Queen's Ferry Press, 2016) and a single book-length poem, titled *The Catamount*, published by Nomadic Press in 2017. Her watercolors illustrate *The Catamount* and *In Case of Emergency, Break Glass.* She holds an MFA in Poetry from Vermont College, and teaches in the Antioch University/LA low-residency MFA program. More of her drawings, short films, and writing can be seen at sarahvanarsdale.com

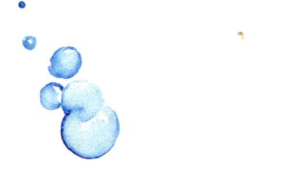

www.ingramcontent.com/pod-product-compliance
Lightning Source LLC
Chambersburg PA
CBHW041952150426

43198CB00005B/109